Bessie Coleman's Story

Tommie Sue Parker, Narrator

By

L.J. Maxie

Topaz Publishing

Reading Entertainment for the Entire Family

Bessie Coleman's Story

Tommie Sue Parker, Narrator

By

L. J. Maxie

All Rights reserved

ISBN-13: 978-0615535197
ISBN-10: 0615535194

Copyright © September 2011 L.J. Maxie

Cover Art Copyright © September 2011 Dawné Dominique,

Topaz Publishing Clip Art Copyright ©dreamstime2011

Editor: Kase J. Reed

This work is based on the life and accomplishments of Bessie Coleman. Every attempt has been made to accurately depict historical facets of her life. Conflicting information may inadvertently occur in this printed document. All rights reserved, including the right to reproduce this book, or portions thereof, in any form.

Publisher:

Topaz Publishing, LLC, USA

Topazpublishingllc.com~ topazpublishing@aol.com

DEDICATION

The Bessie Coleman Aerospace Legacy, Inc.
Living the Legacy
Fly-Sister-Fly

"*Thank you - Mrs. Maxie for inviting readers into the world of 'Queen Bess' through the eyes of Mrs. Tommie Sue Parker. Mrs. Parker's respect for her friend and our shero, Queen Bess, flows throughout your book. The Bessie Coleman Aerospace Legacy, Inc.*

ENDORSEMENTS

Bessie Coleman was the first African American Aviatrix in the United States. An old storyteller narrates accurate historical facts about Coleman's failures and triumphs.

Endorsed by The Bessie Coleman Aerospace Legacy, Inc.

"It looks like a good day to fly!" Thelma Rudd

Sandra J. Campbell, MSM, ATM
Playwright, Storyteller, Reenactor, Professional Speaker, Professor

Melody Cranford
Reenactments of African American Figures in History.
Storyteller & Speaker, Atlanta, Texas

Endorsement: Kathryn Peacock, Educator, and Historian for the town of Atlanta, Texas.

"Bessie Coleman seems to *come alive* in Maxie's oral description of Coleman's friendship with Mrs. Parker. This book is a poignant and entertaining approach to learning for children as well as adults."

ABOUT THE AUTHOR

Atlanta, Texas, the birthplace of Bessie Coleman, is also home for L.J. Maxie. Maxie is an educator, with a Master's degree in education. She is the author of *Stephanie's Emerald Fever*, as well as the stage play production, *The Emerald Fever*. Maxie is a speaker and advocate for Prevention of Family Violence. Available publications include: Stephanie's Emerald Fever, *Cherubs,* a children's book to promote kid safety, Snelly Learns a Lesson, and *Beulah the Butterfly,* a children's book with a focus on behavioral modification. FMI contact: maxie1661@aol.com

Audience: Children, Juvenile, Middle School.
Tags: Aviation, Space, (Early Pioneers), Women's Non-Fiction, African American History, Trailblazers. The Bessie Coleman Aerospace Legacy, Inc.

About
Melody Cranford, Trailblazer
The Legacy Lives On

Atlanta, Texas, is Bessie Coleman's birthplace. Melody Cranford is also native to Atlanta. She labors tirelessly to share Bessie's strength and courage with children and teens.

Sharing her one-woman production depicting Bessie Coleman, Cranford tours schools and visits various organizations. While holding children's attention, Cranford takes her audience from Bessie's childhood to her adulthood, changing costumes right before their very eyes.

Dressed as Bessie, the airplane mechanic, Cranford leads onlookers through several phases of Coleman's life. As Cranford speaks, children are awed. She also includes the plane crash which she so tactfully describes.

Cranford's message is loud and clear. Study hard, believe in yourself, and never give up on your dreams. Outfitted in a replica of Coleman's military style uniform, Cranford also tours festivals.

Introduction

Bessie Coleman was the first African American Aviatrix in the United States. The compelling story of Bessie Coleman has been told many times and by many great authors. However, Mrs. Maxie takes *Bessie's story,* to a new height. The author narrates the story through an old storyteller named Tommie Sue Parker.

Tommie Sue tells Bessie's story in her own words. Using a dialect flavored with a strong Texas twang, Tommie Sue gets her point across. Mrs. Parker claims she met Bessie Coleman on the train headed for Chicago. On that train, she and Bessie became lifelong friends.

Weaving her tale from the cotton fields to the airfields, Tommie Sue provides accurate historical facts about Bessie Coleman's life. Bessie Coleman, a daring African American Aviatrix who succeeded against the odds. Bessie Coleman's Story is entertaining, and informative, capturing the heart as well as the imagination.

Howdy! My name is Mrs. Tommie Sue Parker. Come on in and sit a spell. Right neighborly of you to pay me a visit. Folks 'round here loves to hear me tell stories. I got a heap of stories in this old gray head of mine. …guess that makes me a storyteller.

Right now, my memory is still pretty sharp. First, I'll tell you a little bit 'bout me and why I knows so much 'bout Bessie Coleman.

See, I was born in the Piney Woods of East Texas. I was one of Bessie Coleman's oldest and dearest friends. I guess I knew practically everything 'bout her. I love talking to folks 'bout Bessie, and folks love asking me 'bout her. Now, I'm kinda old, and they say I have a wee bit of a Texas twang, so listen good, ya hear.

Now, where should I start? Oh, I first met Bessie Coleman back in 1915. I was pert near eighteen years old at that time. Mama had done bought me a ticket, so I was sitting on a train headed straight for Chicago, Illinois.

That train pulled into a station, and we was 'bout to pick up some more passengers. Some folks got off the train and some folks got on the train. I had only been on the train for a short spell but it was getting mighty hot. I was a'using my fan to keep me cool.

Now, I wasn't what you call real cute, but I ain't never been real ugly, neither. Well, when I looked up I saw this young lady getting on the train. She was carryin' an old suitcase and it looked a might heavy. I reckon she was 'bout twenty-three years old then, and pretty as a June flower.

My mama said a smile don't cost nothing, so I smiled to show myself friendly. Ain't one to be selfish. I could tell she wanted to sit down, so I scooted over to make room.

"Howdy," I said. "My name is Tommie Sue Parker. I'm on my way to Chicago."

She gave me the prettiest smile I ever did see. After fixin' her dress, she said her name was Bessie Coleman and that she was from Waxahachie, Texas.

I thought that was kinda funny, 'cause I was from the Piney Woods area of North East Texas. That meant we was pert near neighbors. Anyways, it was a long way to Chicago, but we had plenty to talk about. Bessie and I hit it off right away. Pretty soon we started yakking away like we was old friends.

"I'm on my way to Chicago, too," she said. "My two brothers live on the South side. Hopefully, I'm going to find work."

"Land-o-sake," I said. "I'm lookin' for work too. My uncle and aunt said I could probably find work at the laundry. It's a pretty big laundry. They wash hotel sheets, restaurant table cloths and such as that."

Bessie Coleman was somethin' special—I just knew it. She told me all about herself. I remember it like it was yesterday. Now, let's see. Bessie said her parents was named George and Susan Coleman.

That girl was born in a little town just down the road. I believe it's called, Atlanta, Texas. ...come from a real big family. You know, in the 1800's, large families was right common. A family needed every helpin' hand when it comes time for plantin' and harvestin'.

When them Colemans lived in Atlanta, there was nine of them children. But when Bessie was born, she was the tenth child. Now, I always heard, the tenth child was born for luck. Some of that sayin' might be true when it came to that Bessie Coleman.

Like most places in Texas, it was hard to make a living in a small town like Atlanta. To earn a living, the Coleman family worked as sharecroppers. Sharecroppers planted crops on land they didn't own. When it was time to harvest, the crops was shared with the landowner.

While that train rolled right on up the track, we learned a lot about each other that day. Bessie told me that her mama, Susan, was an African American, while George, her daddy, was of Native American descent, yes he was.

He was a mixture of Choctaw, Cherokee Indian, and African American.

That George Coleman was a proud man, but it was hard to get a job in Texas. Back in those days, Texans didn't understand the beliefs or traditions of Native Americans. In other words, what was normal for George, seemed strange to folks from other races.

I believe Bessie said she was born January 26, 1892. When she was birthed, they named her Elizabeth. Ain't that a pretty name? When Elizabeth was a little older, they threw that fancy name clean away, and called her Bessie.

Don't get me wrong, all them Coleman children was special in their own way, but Elizabeth seemed extra special.

Two years after Bessie was birthed, George and Susan got to feeling the strain of being broke. That's when they picked up and moved to Waxahachie, Texas.

To ease financial strain, them Colemans ran a cotton-picking business, yes they did. You know, Bessie loved being outside but she didn't like picking that ole cotton. Most of all,

Bessie liked playing games with her sisters and brothers.

Now, when it came to church, Bessie's family was real Christian-like. Good folks. They went to church every Sunday. Seems, they was always churchin'.

As each of them children grew up, they helped their daddy work in the field, or they found other fields to work in.

Even though Bessie was young, she was smart, clever, and had lots of energy. Oh, she did her chores and helped her mama around the house.

Wouldn't you know it—three more children was birthed after Bessie. She said them children kept her mighty busy.

Sometimes, Bessie would help her mama in the garden, gather eggs, or shell them old dry peas. I hate shellin' peas myself, but Bessie didn't mind. She helped in any way she could.

When Bessie was justa sprout, she would wave goodbye to her brothers and sisters. They was school age, you know, but Bessie was not. That girl could hardly wait for them to get home in the evening.

Every evening Bessie's brothers and sisters would tell her things they learned at that school house. And, Bessie loved learning new things.

One glorious day, Bessie was finally old enough to go to that school house with her brothers and sisters. Wouldn't you know it- that school was far away.

In the late 1800's, there was no sucha thing as a school bus for Bessie's family. Poor little Bessie had to walk to school, even when the weather was mighty bad. Braving cold or hot weather weren't no real problem for little Bessie. She just loved going to school, and didn't care what the weather was like.

Back in those days, most black schools had eight grades, and they was all taught in one room, yes they was. Sometimes the teacher had class huddled right 'round a warm, potbelly stove. Being uncomfortable didn't stop that Bessie Coleman; she was still excited 'bout learnin' and such.

Like most folks in these parts, the school house was poor, too. Chalk for writin' on them fancy chalkboards was scarce as hen's teeth. Sometimes, the white schools gave the black schools their used textbooks. They didn't want them no more because they was old. Some of them books had pages that was missing.

Them children even took turns sharing the same pencil in Bessie's school. Can you imagine that?

Each day, that little Bessie Coleman could hardly wait to get to school. She loved to read them books from the library. After school, that child would almost run home to read stories to her younger sisters and brothers.

Bessie would hurry up and finish her chores, then sit on the porch to read stories 'bout real folks like Booker T. Washington and Harriet Tubman. Reading 'bout these folks helped Bessie. She began to understand that even though she was an African American, she could still become famous someday.

Bessie said, "Tommie Sue, I was good at figuring numbers when I was a little girl. I could figure big numbers right in my head!"

Everybody in Bessie's family was amazed by her mathematical ability. By the age of eight, little Bessie's mama found out that child was truly gifted with them numbers. She got so good with figuring numbers that while the other children worked at the family's business, Bessie worked as the family's bookkeeper. Imagine that!

As the family's bookkeeper, Bessie kept track of all them profits her family made with their cotton pickin' business. She wrote down the amount of cotton that was sold and kept up with the profits that was earned.

Oh, I wouldn't expect nothin' less from that Bessie Coleman. Bessie could accomplish anything once she set her mind to it. She did some pretty amazing things — things most folks thought was plumb near impossible.

Quick as a cat can lick his foot, Bessie completed all eight of them grades and still wanted more schooling. I only got through fifth grade myself, and I was right happy.

All that learning came to an end when it was time for the cotton to be harvested. They shut down all the black schools, while all the white schools stayed open. This was because all African Americans had to pick cotton.

There was no time for singing at church, or doing your own chores. In my home town, even I had to pick cotton. But, that Bessie was always thinking and plannin'. She said that one day things would be different for black folks.

As that train chugged along we looked out the window for a spell. We saw sheep, goats, cows, green meadows, and other towns. A few more other folks got on that train.

Well, I reckon Bessie was getting a might homesick and just felt like talkin'. She said, "Tommie Sue. You're a right friendly sort. I feel comfortable talking to you."

I tried to thank her, but she just went right on talkin' and starin' into space.

Bessie said that in 1901, she was nine years old. Something mighty terrible happened in her life back then. Her daddy got tired of folks pickin' on him. He just got plumb fed up!

Life was hard on the African American, but it was even harder for a Native American.

Bessie's daddy always got treated bad 'cause his skin was a different color. It wasn't black, and it wasn't white, it was red!

That old George Coleman felt the folks in Texas would never accept him. He wanted to go back home. Ain't it nice to go back home when you feel picked on?

In the Oklahoma Indian Territory George would be treated with kindness and respect. The way folks should be treated. George felt that gettin' a job would be easier in Oklahoma.

Naturally, he begged his wife to go with him to Oklahoma, but she wouldn't. Just as George felt unaccepted in Texas, I reckon she felt Oklahoma would be no kinder to an African American.

Bessie said, one day her daddy just jumped-up. He left his wife and all them children in Texas. He moved back to Oklahoma to get a real good job.

Now, Bessie was plumb sick about this. She loved her daddy and missed him sorely.

Her mama found it pert near impossible to make ends meet without her husband. She worked hard, and like a good child, Bessie helped.

To make money, they cleaned up folks homes and took in all the laundry they could wash. Bessie was pretty good size when she started working on jobs and saving her own money.

Knowing folks thought African Americans weren't book smart, she would need more education if she ever wanted to amount to anything.

Before Bessie boarded that train headed for Chicago, she decided she was going to put herself through college. …used all her little savings and enrolled in college. It was called, Oklahoma Colored Agricultural and Normal

University. Now, this same college is known as Langston University in Langston Oklahoma.

Bessie learned that college is very expensive. That child soon ran clean out of money. Once again, she walked around with her face draggin' the ground. Her dreams of a college education didn't look like it was ever going to come true.

Bessie had to go back home to Waxahachie, Texas. In a way, Bessie was much like her daddy. She knew that an African American wouldn't be able to find work in her home town. No sir, she needed to move to a bigger city if she wanted to find her some work.

And, that's when I met *The- Bessie Coleman*. We was two young black women, running from a nightmare and searching for a dream.

Chicago, Illinois was a large city — still is! It was bustling with tall buildings that nearly touched the sky. It had lots of jobs and industries. Plus, in Chicago, African Americans was treated a little bit better. Bessie felt she would have a better chance of finding work there, and I agreed.

When we got off that train in Chicago, I promised Bessie I would keep in touch with her. I thanked her for the company and went on my way. Every now and again, we saw each other, and sometimes we didn't see each other for a spell.

As time passed, Bessie turned into a stunnin' young woman. I didn't look too bad myself, but I didn't hold a candle to that Bessie Coleman. She never did lose sight of her dreams to become successful, so she took on jobs and continued to work hard.

Now, when Bessie was twenty-three, she worked as a manicurist at the White Sox Barber Shop. Them mens and women loved how nice she made they fingers look. As you know, Bessie was always going to do her very best. She became known as the fastest manicurist in all Chicago — even had her picture right there in the newspaper.

Lots of important folks came in and out of that barber shop. They would get their hair cut or get their shoes shined. Every now and again, they would get a quick manicure from Bessie.

Mostly, folks didn't come in the shop to spend money. They came in the barber shop just to chew the fat. They swapped tales and told stories about politics and war.

One day, Bessie came to my house. She was a frightful mess, a'bawlin' and a'squallin' 'cause they done sent her two brothers off to the war.

That Bessie was so worried, she was reading everything to find out if her brothers were okay. Then one day she told me, "Tommie Sue. I've been reading a lot 'bout the war. They have war heroes who fly airplanes on dangerous missions. I wish I could do something like that."

Just the thought of being up in the sky with no safety nets makes my liver quiver. But not Bessie, she had nerves of steel.

When Bessie's brothers came home from the war, that Bessie was on top of the world. Right away, her brothers started talking 'bout how them French women was smarter than us American women. They said French women was so quick they could even fly airplanes.

Well, that was all Bessie needed to hear. She was already plumb crazy 'bout them planes. That Bessie sopped up them stories like homemade sorghum on a hot butter-biscuit! Just the thought of becoming a pilot and flyin' one of them airplanes had put that girl's head in the wind.

One of them brothers told Bessie that dreaming 'bout becoming an aviator was slap crazy! Not only was Bessie an African American, but she was also a woman.

Folks thought African American women couldn't do nothing but clean houses, cook, and do laundry. Nobody believed an African American woman would ever pilot one of them airplanes.

Bessie got tired of being teased 'bout flying one of them planes. Somehow, that boy's doubt only made Bessie stronger. She was never going to give up on that dream, ever!

Bless her lucky stars, Bessie met a man by the name of Robert Abbot. Abbot was a right smart sort. He was the founder and publisher of a newspaper called, *The Chicago Defender*, yes he was.

Abbot used that newspaper to encourage African Americans. ... told them to be proud of who they was. ...hold up they head and get a education. Then he said, set you some goals, then work toward them goals. Bessie musta been listening, 'cause that's exactly what she did. She worked all kinds of jobs and saved her money.

Bessie also met Jesse Binga. Now, Binga was the founder of Binga State Bank. Just like usual, Bessie was always doing her best. Abbot and Binga saw that Bessie wasn't no lazy woman. Folks don't mind helpin' you if you work hard. Hard work catches folks' eyes. They decided to help her go to flight school by giving her the money she needed.

Although Bessie Coleman was a pretty young thing, and had an outgoing personality, no one in America would let her attend they flight schools. No matter how bright or well-spoken Bessie was, she was still a black woman. And, no body was going to train a black woman to fly! Ain't that a shame?

Bessie told me she didn't want to give up on her dreams to fly one of them airplanes. I told her to ask Robert Abbott what to do 'cause he was a smart man. Abbot told Bessie to go to Paris France. He said a woman could learn how to fly in Paris.

Bessie got all excited 'bout going to France, but she didn't speak no French. That didn't stop old Bessie. She started studyin' French at that Berltiz School in Chicago. ...got pretty good at it too. I didn't know what she was sayin, but it sounded a might pretty.

On November 20, 1920 Bessie took her first trip to Paris. She was finally on her way toward fulfilling them dreams of hers. In

France, she learned how to fly what they called a Nieuport plane, yes she did! At that flying school, they taught Bessie how to do tail spins, looping the loop and banking.

On June 15, 1921, Bessie Coleman became the first African American woman to earn her aviation pilot's license in the world, yes she did! She also got a international aviation license. I was proud of Bessie Coleman and her folks was proud of her, too.

But, something was still ailing Bessie. Although she could fly, she wanted to become a better pilot. Now, she felt like she needed more of them flying lessons. I would have been happy just learnin' to drive a motor car. But not Bessie, she wanted to be the finest pilot ever! That Bessie took lessons from a French ace pilot near Paris. In September, she returned to New York.

Bessie had accomplished only part of her dream. She said, "Tommie Sue, I can't make no money flying in the United States, but I can make money entertaining folks as a stunt flyer."

So, as it was, Bessie decided she would perform dangerous stunts in the sky to entertain folks. Large crowds would pay to see an African American woman fly a plane.

And, Bessie was right. Because she wanted to be the best pilot ever, she took even more of them flying lessons. Even though Bessie had earned them flying licenses, fair and square, nobody would teach her what she wanted to know.

Then, Bessie sailed to Europe in February of 1922. She completed more of them advance classes in aviation. That Bessie Coleman wanted even more knowledge, so she went on to Holland.

While she was in Holland, Bessie met this important man called, Anthony Fokker. Fokker was real famous for designing them aircrafts. After a while, Bessie went on to Germany to get more training. She even learned how to do minor repairs to fix them airplanes if somethin' went wrong.

When Bessie returned to the United States she was spit polished and ready! As proud as Bessie was, she was going to show the world just how talented she had become. Bessie had designed a fancy military-style flight uniform. Only Bessie could wear something like that. It was right purty.

On September 3, 1922, Bessie had her first air show, and I was standing right there cheering her on. Now, the purpose of that show was to honor African American World War Veterans.

Robert Abbott was so excited, he wrote an article in his newspaper to tell everybody Bessie Coleman was the greatest African American woman stunt pilot in the world. Eight other pilots was also featured at that Checkerboard Airdrome air show.

If I must say so myself, Bessie's show was like nothing I'd ever did see! ...made the hair stand up on the back of my neck, yes it did! While I was standing there with my mouth open, Bessie did daredevil stunts and loops.

She flew so close to the ground you could almost touch that plane. Lands sake!

The crowd went crazy for Bessie's fancy flying! Before you knew it, Bessie became famous over night! Just like one of them movie stars.

Almost everybody had heard of Elizabeth *'Bessie'* Coleman. Pretty soon, she became popular all over the United States. The newspapers called her **'Brave Bessie'** and **'Queen Bess'**.

I was standing right there when the newspaper folks interviewed her, sure was.

Bessie didn't talk like me at all. All that education gave Bessie confidence. She spoke right up and told them all 'bout herself.

Black folks and whites folks admired my friend, Bessie Coleman. She performed in a heap of air shows after that. Nearly scared old Tommie Sue to death every time she crashed, but she always walked away.

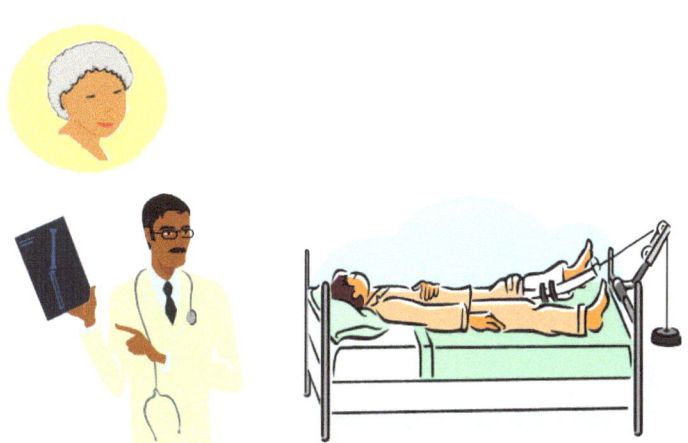

On February 22, 1922, Bessie flew in an airshow, in Los Angeles California. That girl broke three of her ribs and her leg when that plane crashed. Surely, I thought this was Bessie's last flight. But you know what? Bessie told her fans she wouldn't let no plane crash stop her from flying.

Believe it or not, Bessie flew them JN-4 Jenny Biplanes and them army surplus planes. You know, the ones left over from the war. And, for the next five years Bessie thrilled crowds of folks with her fancy flying.

Even these accomplishments was not enough to satisfy old Bessie. There was one more thing she wanted to do. I just couldn't figure out what more she wanted. I woulda been glad just to have my picture in the paper.

She was already the top woman stunt flyer in the United States. Well, little did I know, Bessie wanted to become a professional aviator and wouldn't stop at nothing to do stunts that was even more difficult.

'bout this time, Bessie was offered a leading role in a movie called *Shadow and the Sunshine*. When she told me 'bout that movie, we both jumped up and down like little children. I had never known no movie star before, so this was exciting news.

Bessie said, "Tommy Sue, this movie can boost my flying career and I can make a whole lotta money."

I thought she was pretty much right with her thinking. But when Bessie learned they wanted her to play a poor old ignorant black girl who went to the big city, Bessie said, "I just can't do it, Tommie Sue. There is no way I'm going to play the part of an ignorant black girl. I've worked too hard to educate myself. That movie could make my entire race look bad."

Dang it, if Bessie wasn't right again. Life for blacks was hard enough. She didn't want to star in no movie that made folks think all blacks was stupid. As a black woman, Bessie had faced a whole buncha hitches. No sir, she just couldn't erase the trail she had blazed for women.

Bessie upheld African Americans everywhere when she refused that role, and walked off that fancy movie set.

Meanwhile Bessie had other dreams she was workin' on, yes she did. She had her eye set on opening a school for young black aviators. You know what? Bessie never did finish that dream.

If my memory serves me, Bessie was 34 years old when she bought a plane in Dallas, to fly in an air show. Now, this plane had just been flown to Jacksonville, Florida. They had to land it three times 'cause it wasn't running right. That plane gave Bessie's family a bad taste of the jitters. They didn't feel that plane was safe enough for Bessie's performance.

At that time, William Wills was Bessie's publicity agent and mechanic. On the morning of April 30, 1926 Bessie and Wills took that plane out for a test flight before the air show. Wills flew that plane while Bessie sat in the passenger's seat. I reckon she sat in the passenger's seat so she could check out the terrain for a parachute jump. Bessie didn't bother to put on no seatbelt neither, she needed to look out the side of that plane to see the ground.

Luckily, I wasn't there. They tell me that ten minutes into that flight, that plane didn't pull out of a planned nosedive. Instead, that plane went into a nasty tail spin. Poor Bessie was thrown from that plane and didn't survive. William Wills couldn't get control of that plane, it crashed and burned. Bless his heart, Wills didn't survive neither.

Tell me, that plane was crumpled up and burnt up something awful. Finally, they found out what made that plane crash. The wrench used to service that engine had slid into what they call the gearbox. Jammed that thing right on up! And that's what caused Elizabeth 'Bessie' Coleman's plane to crash.

It was a sad day for Bessie's family. 5,000 mourners attended Bessie's funeral services. It was estimated that 10,000 people walked past her coffin all day and night. Later on, Bessie was buried in the Lincoln Cemetery.

After her death, Bessie Coleman Aero Clubs started popping up all over the place. Lieutenant William J. Powell promoted the cause of black aviation through his writings and using the Bessie Coleman Aero Club.

Oh, the world didn't forget 'bout my friend Bessie. On Labor Day 1931, these clubs held the first all African American Air Show. Each year, they fly over the Lincoln Cemetery to honor my friend, Queen Bess.

Now, Bessie was inducted into the Texas Aviation Hall of Fame in 2000. And in 1995 the United State Postal Department issued a Bessie Coleman postage stamp. Imagine that! I got to know Bessie pretty good. Her motto was never give up.

From the cotton fields to the airfields Elizabeth 'Bessie' Coleman blazed a trail for African Americans and women everywhere.

I hope you enjoyed this story 'bout my friend, Bessie. Now, ya'll come back to see me again, ya hear. Tommie Sue Parker, Storyteller

My Friend, Bessie Coleman

Bessie Coleman Facts

NAME: Elizabeth (Bessie) Coleman

DATE OF BIRTH: January 26, 1892

PLACE OF BIRTH: Atlanta, Texas

FAMILY BACKGROUND: Bessie was the tenth of thirteen children born to Susan and George Coleman. Her father was one-quarter African-American and three-quarters Choctaw and Cherokee Indian. Her mother was African-American.
The family settled in Waxahachie, Texas when Coleman was two years old, and ran a business for picking cotton.
In 1915 Coleman moved to Chicago, Illinois

EDUCATION: After high school, Coleman enrolled in the Colored Agricultural and Normal University in Langston, Oklahoma completing one term.

Bessie Coleman Facts

NAME: Elizabeth (Bessie) Coleman

DATE OF BIRTH: January 26, 1892

PLACE OF BIRTH: Atlanta, Texas

FAMILY BACKGROUND: Bessie was the tenth of thirteen children born to Susan and George Coleman. Her father was one-quarter African-American and three-quarters Choctaw and Cherokee Indian. Her mother was African-American.
The family settled in Waxahachie, Texas when Coleman was two years old, and ran a business for picking cotton.
In 1915 Coleman moved to Chicago, Illinois

EDUCATION: After high school, Coleman enrolled in the Colored Agricultural and Normal University in Langston, Oklahoma completing one term.

ACCOMPLISHMENTS:

On June 15, 1921, Bessie received her pilot's license from the renowned Federation Aeronautique Internationale.

Coleman left for France in November, 1920. In seven months, she completed the ten-month course at the Ecole d'Aviation des Freres Caudon at Le Crotoy in the Somme.

Coleman learned to fly in a French Nieuport Type 82, including "tail spins, banking, and looping the loop."

Coleman was the first licensed black pilot in the U.S.

Coleman was the first American to obtain her pilot's license from the French Aviation School. After studying for an additional three months in France, Coleman returned to the U.S.

On September 3, 1922, Coleman gave her first performance at an air show at Curtiss Field, near New York City.

Coleman became famous; known as Queen Bess or Brave Bessie.

Coleman began a movie career, but broke her contract with the movie company. She felt the role was demeaning to women.

Coleman flew a war surplus JN-4 ("Jenny") army trainer plane. It stalled on the first flight and crashed. Bessie received broken ribs and a broken leg.

DATE OF DEATH: April 30, 1926

April 30, Coleman and her mechanic took the JN-4 Jenny plane for a test run. It malfunctioned, the mechanic lost control. Bessie was not wearing a seatbelt to check the terrain for a parachute jump. The plane suddenly accelerated and flipped over. Coleman was thrown from the plane. The plane crashed killing the pilot.

PLACE OF DEATH: Jacksonville, Florida

Thousands of people mourned Bessie's death -- from Jacksonville and Orlando to Chicago. Three funerals were held; one in each of those cities. An estimated 10,000 people paid their last respects at the memorial in Chicago. Coleman was buried at Lincoln Cemetery.

On September 3, 1922, Coleman gave her first performance at an air show at Curtiss Field, near New York City.

Coleman became famous; known as Queen Bess or Brave Bessie.

Coleman began a movie career, but broke her contract with the movie company. She felt the role was demeaning to women.

Coleman flew a war surplus JN-4 ("Jenny") army trainer plane. It stalled on the first flight and crashed. Bessie received broken ribs and a broken leg.

DATE OF DEATH: April 30, 1926

April 30, Coleman and her mechanic took the JN-4 Jenny plane for a test run. It malfunctioned, the mechanic lost control. Bessie was not wearing a seatbelt to check the terrain for a parachute jump. The plane suddenly accelerated and flipped over. Coleman was thrown from the plane. The plane crashed killing the pilot.

PLACE OF DEATH: Jacksonville, Florida

Thousands of people mourned Bessie's death -- from Jacksonville and Orlando to Chicago. Three funerals were held; one in each of those cities. An estimated 10,000 people paid their last respects at the memorial in Chicago. Coleman was buried at Lincoln Cemetery.

Important Dates & Facts

1929, Lt. William J. Powell founded the Bessie Coleman Aero Club

1931, The Challenger Pilots' Association of Chicago, first annual flyover above Lincoln Cemetery, in honor of Coleman.

1934, Powell dedicated his book *Black Wings* to her memory.

1977, Women pilots in the Chicago region founded the Bessie Coleman Aviators Club.

1990, A road near Chicago's O'Hare Airport was renamed Bessie Coleman Drive,

Chicago declares May 2, 1992, Bessie Coleman Day.

1995, the U.S. Postal Department issued the Bessie Coleman stamp. Inducted into the Women in Aviation Hall of Fame.

2000, Bessie Coleman was inducted into the Texas Aviation Hall of Fame.

2006 Bessie Coleman inducted into the National Aviation Hall of Fame, Dayton, Ohio - Class of 2006.

WEB SITES:

Women in History. Bessie Coleman biography. Lakewood Public Library. <http://www.lkwdpl.org/wihohio/cole-bes.htm>.

BessieColeman.com - Well done website by Luke Irvin

Bessie Coleman - Gale Free Resources - Black History Month

National Women's Hall of Fame

World's first African-American woman pilot honored with U.S. Stamp by Agnes Barr, The Ninety-Nines International Organization of Women Pilots

Aeronautics - Bessie Coleman - Allstar Network profile

Bessie Coleman (1896-1926) - Early Illinois Women